L E   M A N S

PORSCHE

LE MANS

PORSCHE

JOHN S ALLEN

Acknowledgements

My thanks for help in obtaining additional material for this book go to photographers Ken Wells and David Cundy, and to Klaus Parr, keeper of Porsche's archives. Assistance has been kindly provided by Monique Bouleux and the Service de Presse of the Automobile Club de l'Ouest, Dave and Lorraine Morse and their enthusiastic co-workers in the Porsche Club of America, and Dale Miller of the Collier Automotive Museum, Naples, Florida. Thanks also go to Bruce Canepa for information on his delectable stable of racing Porsches, and to FISA's Laurent Chetrit for facilities provided at Le Mans and elsewhere. Thank you also to everyone at Osprey, who make such a good job of putting everything together.

John S Allen

Published in 1992 by Osprey Publishing 59 Grosvenor Street, London W1X 9DA

A catalogue record for this book is available from the British Library

ISBN 185532204 8

Editor Shaun Barrington
Page design Jessica Caws
Printed in Hong Kong

Front cover
Moby Dick, the Great White Whale, had, like so many experimental Porsches, only a one-season life. This, the 935/78, was the ultimate development of the works 935 programme, and was powered by a 3.2-litre 740bhp version of the venerable 911 motor. At Le Mans 1978 the drivers of chassis 007, the only example built, were Rolf Stommelen and Manfred Schurti; they finished eighth overall. Note the deep endplates on the transverse wing; it appears that Porsche started with these plates longer than was expected to be necessary, and intended to experiment to find out how short they could be and still be effective. However, so much time and effort was spent on getting the engine right that the wing endplates never were investigated properly, and so remained unchanged. (Photo courtesy Porsche)

Right
Many enthusiasts agree that the Shell/Dunlop colours worn by the 1988 Works 962s were amongst the most attractive ever seen on racing Porsches. This car is 962 010, which at Le Mans was driven by Derek Bell, Hans Stuck and Klaus Ludwig. Having been delayed with fuel pick-up problems, it came within half a lap of catching the Jaguar which won that year's event. Subsequently, 010 was passed on to Kremer Racing, who never raced it, but instead displayed it prominently in the showroom of their Köln premises. It was then sold to American Frank Gallogly, who brought it to the Laguna Seca gathering

Half title page
924 003 was one of a trio of similar cars which the factory entered at Le Mans 1980. Each was decorated with a national flag blended in to the design, this car being the American one (the others were British and German) in honour of its drivers, Pete Gregg and Al Holbert. The Germans finished sixth overall, the Brits twelfth, and the Americans came in at thirteenth

Title page
It's the lull before the storm. Work on the cars has stopped, and they are lined up en épi in front of the pits. The pre-race atmosphere at Le Mans is electric, and anyone who has not yet experienced it should do so as soon as possible

For a catalogue of all books published by Osprey Automotive please write to:

The Marketing Department, Octopus Illustrated Books, 1st Floor, Michelin House, 81 Fulham Road, London SW3 6RB

Contents

Introduction

One week after the dust from Le Mans 1990 had settled, the Porsche Club of America held its 35th Annual Porsche Parade. The twin venues for the event were Monterey and Laguna Seca, and the highlight of the week's activities was a remarkable gathering of Le Mans Porsches, a colourful tribute to the race cars which have worked so hard to give Porsche its unequalled reputation.

The Porsche Parade's Tribute to Porsche at Le Mans provided the inspiration for this book – an affectionate look at the many types of Porsches which have, over forty-one years, become synonymous with Le Mans.

This book is also a (personal) tribute of a different kind – a requiem for that most entertaining of institutions: the Le Mans paddock. It has for many years been a meeting place, a hive of activity, and a fascinating display area in which members of the public could rub shoulders with the people who have put their hearts and souls into making sports car racing successful, and where they could see and photograph in close-up the World's fastest racing cars being prepared for battle.

In the week leading up to the big race, the openness of the paddock encouraged all and sundry, including the author, to encounter the reality of racing cars, in a manner which was impossible at any other circuit. More than a few team members were understandably less than happy with the proximity of the public, but for the fans it was pure joy. But now it has gone, 1990 being the last year of the fascinating Parc des Ravitaillements. Modernisation of the circuit's pits complex has instead given teams the privacy and security of shuttered and lockable pit garages which are rapidly becoming a standard part of motor racing everywhere.

Nonetheless, Le Mans remains the pinnacle of sportscar racing; long may it continue to be.

If this book has a third purpose, it may be to provide answers to some of the questions of the ubiquitous modellers who now permeate the racing scene, and who repeatedly come to the author with queries which go something like: 'You were at Le Mans in '74 weren't you? What colour was Porsche number ...?'

For political reasons, the works Porsche team boycotted Le Mans 1984. Whilst the works cat was away, the privateer mice went out to play. The marque's reputation was in good hands, as Porsche were fully aware. When the Lancia threat had fallen apart, the private teams went at each other hammer and tongs, and when it was all over the laurels went to Joest Racing, whose 956 117 was driven by Henri Pescarolo and Klaus Ludwig. Porsches occupied all the places from first to seventh, plus ninth. Who needs a works team when you have customers like those?

Lies, Damn' Lies, and...

Statistics seem very appropriate to the story of Porsches at Le Mans. What should be established at the outset is precisely what is meant by a Porsche, and in this context a Porsche is considered to be any car which raced under that name, although, latterly, several of the Porsche 962s which have contested the Le Mans 24-Hours have, in fact, been assembled around what may be termed 'pirate' chassis. Excluded from these statistics are Porsche-powered vehicles such as the Kremer CK-5, some Cougars, and the March-Porsches, because they were entered under names other than Porsche.

It all began at 4pm on 23 June, 1951, when the pits straight at the Circuit Permanent de La Sarthe saw sixty cars set off on the 19th edition of les 24 Heures du Mans, then, and arguably still now, the most prestigious and important motor race in the world. Amongst the sixty hopefuls was a single car from a then little-known German team, Porsche. The silver car was a diminutive coupé, powered by a 1086cc flat-four engine, and driven by two Frenchmen, Auguste Veuillet and E Mouche. After 24 hours of racing, the plumply rounded Porsche crossed the finish line in twentieth position.

Forty years later, there were rather more Porsches taking part in the 24 Hours of Le Mans, and they also managed a better result: 7th overall. In every one of those 41 years from 1951 to 1991, Porsches took part in the classic French race, and in the process notched up no less than twelve victories, to become unquestionably the most successful Le Mans cars ever. There have been road cars, such as the ubiquitous 911, and even the luxurious 928. There have been dedicated racers, like the awesome 917 and the clinically efficient 956, and there have been so many in between the two extremes.

Stuttgart dedication to the 24-hour grind has resulted in a tally of entries which at times beggars belief, and which can only be seen in context when compared numerically with the competition. Take, for example, the ultimate set of numbers: the number of Porsches which have seen the start of the Grand Prix d'Endurance. In 41 years no fewer than 545 Porsches (plus one which shouldn't have been there, and which was quickly sent packing) have taken the start, those 545 representing 25% of the total entry (2173) of all makes within that period. Needless to say, no other manufacturer can even come close to that tally. Indeed, no other manufacturer has contested 41 consecutive Le Mans events, and it will be many years before anyone else can even approach that number of entries or consecutive races.

Back in 1951, only one Porsche was on the grid. It finished, thus creating a 100% finishing record, and it did so at an average speed of 73.55mph, which for an under-1100cc road-car was an excellent achievement. It could hardly be expected that the same finishing record could be maintained in future years, and when 1952 rolled around, the best the marque could manage was one finisher out of three starters. However, the number of starters grew steadily over the

The Carrera GTL Abarth was unusual in that its stylish aluminium body was built not by Porsche, but by Zagato. Abarth came into the picture basically as middleman, fitting bodies to chassis, because Zagato's dealings with Porsche's competitors made it (for Zagato) politically unwise to be seen to be building bodies for Porsche. The chassis used was pure 356B, and a total of twenty of these 1588cc cars was contracted for. They were much lighter than the 356 Carreras they were intended to replace, had less frontal area and less drag, and competed at Le Mans each year from 1960 to 1962; the best result obtained from the six starts was Edgar Barth's and Hans Herrmann's seventh position, in 1962; this is the car from Porsche's museum, chassis number 1018. (Photo courtesy Porsche)

Lining up for the start of Le Mans 1968, the Porsche fleet waits in the pits. That year, the race was held in September, not June, and the start was at 3pm. The massed ranks of 908s (numbered 31 to 34) and 907s (35, 66 and 67) looked invincible, but weren't. Still, second and third places showed that Porsche was going in the right direction, and that the win could not be far away

years, and by the time 1953 arrived, Porsche was entering not only its type 356 road-cars, but also its first dedicated sports-racers, the type 550.

Overall placings improved dramatically, as the sports-racers were more able to compete with the likes of Ferrari, and in 1958 the Porsche stable netted a 3rd place finish, an extremely creditable achievement for cars which were small-engined and of very low power when compared with the competition. In 1959, there was, unfortunately, a hiccough which mars an otherwise brilliant record: for the first and only time, no Porsche finished the 24-hours. Six cars – five 718s and a single 550 – had been entered, and all retired. The depths were very nearly plumbed one more time, in 1963, but a single survivor managed to make it to the line.

Clearly, there is safety in numbers, and from the arrival of the first mid-engined Porsches, the 1964 type 904, the Le Mans entry list has bulged with Porsches. Seven entries in 1964, 1965 and 1966, then 10 in 1967, before peaking with a massive 33 in 1971. The 1971 race would have been a dull affair were it not for Porsche, who provided 67% of the 49-car field. Of the 33 Porsches, 18 were 911s, a type which had debuted in 1966, and which subsequently became the mainstay of the various GT categories, until in 1975 they alone accounted for 24 of the race's 55 starters, of which 49% were Porsches.

Recent changes in Group C sports-car racing, shifting emphasis on to what are effectively two-seat covered-wheel Formula One cars, have revived that old subject: what, precisely, is the raison d'être of the Le Mans 24-hour race? Some argue that it should be helping in the development of the finest possible road cars, a role which Porsche always supported. There was once a time when normal road cars could be prepared for the track, and compete in the world's greatest race, but sadly this is now a thing of the past. Typifying the road car theme is this 914/6, which was amongst 33 Porsches taking part in the 1971 event. G Quist and D Krumm drove the Autohaus Max Moritz car, which steadily climbed from 37th place at the start, up to 15th position, until gearbox failure forced their retirement

Right
The start of the 1969 edition of the Vingt-quatre Heures du Mans, with Porsches taking all the top places on the grid, 917s netting the first two. The red cars are Ferrari 312Ps, one of which retired after striking debris from the first-lap accident which destroyed John Woolfe's privately entered (but works-prepared) 917. Of the cars visible in this view, taken from the Tribune Citroën opposite the pits, only number 64, on the extreme right, survived to the finish of a race which saw a remarkable level of attrition. The attendance at the 1969 event was incredible, and towards the end of the race the roads to the circuit were jammed with people who had been watching on television, but wanted to be present at the finish of what was proving to be the most exciting ever Le Mans race

Left
*Pedro Rodriguez and Jack Oliver shared
the other JW Automotive langheck at
Le Mans 1971. Alas, 917 043's Le Mans
ended with the rupture of an oil line.
Note the concave surface of the nose of
the car, assisting in the production of
downforce. With the 917 capable of
achieving hitherto unheard-of speeds,
Porsche had to do a great deal of
aerodynamic work to permit the car to
realise its full potential, and the results of
this work can often be seen in the
shapes of cars from other manufacturers*

By the time the last 911 took to the Sarthe circuit, the type had made an almost unbelievable contribution totalling 135 starts – and that figure does not include the turbocharged 930, 934 and 935s derived from the 911. Eventually, the role of the 911 was taken over by the 930, 934 and 935; in 1980 the latter type provided 15 starters, out of a combined Porsche contingent of 24, just 44% of the field, whilst in the period 1976 to 1984, the three versions together mustered just 101 starts.

In 1984 the 40% mark was surpassed for a final time, when Porsches accounted for 22 starters out of 53. Main constituents of the Porsche cohorts in that year were the 956 and its near-identical sister, the 962, between them providing 16 starters. 1984 was the last time that Porsches provided over 20 starters, for from then on the race's emphasis was put squarely on to the sports-prototypes, with the road-going 911s and their derivatives being phased out as more Group C cars became available.

Porsche's growing number of entries resulted, predictably, in an ever increasing number of finishers. Porsche reliability became almost legendary, and the combination of strength and numbers resulted in the make's most impressive showing, which came in 1971: 13 cars finished; 10 of them were Porsches. In the previous year, Porsche gave up only two places to other cars; a mere 7 cars, 5 of them Porsches, were classified as finishing one of the most arduous events ever, a race in which many of the entrants did struggle through appalling weather to reach the finish, but covering insufficient distance to be classified in the final results.

Below

Yet another imposter 917, this time one seen when in the old Musée de l'Automobile du Mans; *it has since taken up residence in the fabulous new museum building which houses some exceptionally imaginative and well-displayed exhibits, and a visit to which is an essential part of any trip to Le Mans. The car is 917 045, formerly a JW Automotive Gulf-sponsored Le Mans racer. It has been restored in the Martini markings of 917 042 which raced at Le Mans in 1971; close comparison of this photograph with pictures of 042, 043 and 045 at Le Mans will prove that the switch in markings has indeed taken place, as all three Le Mans 1971* langhecke *had detail differences in such areas as air-intakes, headlight covers and so on. Modellers should note that the dark blue paintwork at the extreme front of the car is incorrect; it should be black*

From 1951 to 1991, 784 cars have been classified as finishers; Porsche's share was 251, some 32% – almost one in three finishers has been a Porsche. It is small wonder that the make has been so popular with entrants, and why Porsches have become so inextricably linked with the race, particularly when one remembers that out of 545 starts, 251 – nearly half – were finishers.

Nobody expected the very first Porsche Le Mans car to do very well. After all, it was underpowered, and alone. To end up as it did, 20th out of 30 finishers, was something of a surprise. Over the next four years, results improved dramatically. 11th, 15th, 12th, then a superb 4th, giving Porsche a result to be proud of. After the 1959 débâcle, Porsche never again failed to feature in the top ten positions, and from 1968 to 1990 always achieved 4th or better.

The string of wins began in 1970, and was continued with victories in 1971, 1976, 1977, 1979, 1981, 1982, 1983, 1984, 1985, 1986 and 1987. The total of 12 wins puts Porsche well ahead of nearest rivals Ferrari (9), Jaguar (7), Bentley (5), Ford and Alfa Romeo (4 each). Six of Ferrari's victories were consecutive, but Porsche can claim seven such wins (1981 to 1987). Since the inception of the 24-Hours, Porsche has also achieved what is, by a wide margin, the best record of placings. Porsche has 42 placings (ie first to third) against Ferrari's 26 and Jaguar's 15; this shows strength in depth, not only as outright winners.

The cars which did most of Porsche's winning were the 956 and its clone the 962. By 1991 this particular family had been represented on the Le Mans starting grid no fewer than 126 times – the enormity of that number is easier to appreciate when compared with the number of starts recorded by the other great sports-racers of the post-war years: Jaguar's D-Type (26), the Ferrari

There were times when it seemed as if the 908, in one form or another, would go on forever. Escuderia Montjuich entered this chocolate-bar example in 1973, the year of the Le Mans cinquantenaire, 1923-1973. The 908/03 (this is chassis 013) was not intended for night racing, but the afterthought headlamps have been very well blended into the front of the car. Spaniard Juan Fernandez shared the driving with fellow Iberian Franco Torredemer and Swiss Bernard Chenevière; they finished fifth, but were beaten by a works/Martini Carrera RSR. The Porsche 908/03 was a well balanced car, and of this example's scrutineered weight of 741kg, 417kg (some 56%) was on the back wheels

Left

1974, and the 908 is still there. This time it's an /02, chassis 016, entered by Christian Poirot and driven by the entrant and Jean Rondeau, the latter eventually becoming famous for being the first man to achieve a Le Mans win whilst driving a car bearing his own name. This 1969 car was perhaps a little past its prime, and a whole list of problems conspired to prevent it from finishing any higher than 19th

Below

Swiss André Wicky was a Le Mans regular who had first raced at the Sarthe in 1960. His 908/02 spyder was of the type known as the 'Sole' or 'Flounder' because of its flattened appearance, the bodywork between the front and rear fenders being higher and smoother than on the first 908/02 spyders. Wicky's car, driven in 1974 by Frenchmen 'Novestille', (Louis Cosson?) Jacques Boucart and the owner, featured an unusual air outlet set into the nose, a modification not taken up elsewhere. Their 908 retired when the gearbox broke

Testa Rossa (29), and the steel-chassis Ford GT40 and Mirage (40). Furthermore, the number of 956/962s produced by the factory and its authorised agents has now topped 130, and at the time of writing the allegedly final example, 962 177, had made its first race appearance – appropriately enough, at Le Mans. That makes the 956/962 easily the highest production Le Mans sports-racer, well ahead of the D-Type and Testa Rossa, and even edging out the GT40. Allegedly the final car because on two previous occasions Porsche has built a last 962, only to keep the old warhorse in production to satisfy continuing customer orders; it could, conceivably, happen again.

Not only has the 956/962 become the most prolific-ever purpose-built Le Mans car, its quota of wins (6, consecutive) is also a record for any individual type of car. The Jaguar D-Type managed it three times, as did the Ford GT40, whilst the Ferrari Testa Rossa notched up four wins. In 1957 the five Jaguar D-Types entered netted places 1, 2, 3, 4 and 6, but even this performance cannot match the astonishing Porsche achievement of 1983, when nine of the first ten finishers were Porsches – only 9th place escaped the grasp of the 956s; add to that an eleventh place recorded by a type 930, and never was domination of Le Mans so utter.

Porsches have recorded some impressive overall average speeds in their quest for superiority at the Sarthe. The first car's 73.55mph was commendable enough, but it was not until 1958 that a Porsche managed to average a speed in excess of 100mph for the entire duration of the race. The car was the Behra/Herrmann RSK Spyder, chassis 718 005, and its average speed, inclusive of pit-stops, was 101.22mph. Another speed mark was passed in 1967, when the 5th place 907 of Siffert and Herrmann at last broke the 200kph barrier, their 201.273kph being equivalent to 125.07mph.

It was in 1971 that Porsche really made its mark upon the pages of the record books. That year, the winning 917K of Helmut Marko and Gijs van Lennep covered a record distance of 5335.313km in the space of 24 hours, achieving in the process an average speed of 138.13mph, a mark which has not yet been surpassed, although in 1988 a Jaguar missed by only 2.53km. The inclusion, from 1990, of two chicanes on the ligne droite des Hunaudières (the Mulsanne Straight) makes it unlikely that Porsche's speed and distance records will be broken in the next few years.

Porsche's history at Le Mans is one of numbers – vast numbers of entries, and just as large proportions of finishers. Porsche has supported les 24 Heures du Mans in a way unequalled by any other marque, and we can but hope that after 1991, when the 962 is finally laid to rest, a victim of the same sort of rule-changes which dealt the death-blow to the awesome 917, that Porsche will have something with which to replace it. At the time of writing – June 1991 – it appears that Le Mans 1992 will see not a single Porsche aligned for the start, and that the 41-year unbroken run will come to an end; it must be hoped that rule-changes as yet unannounced will somehow permit the inclusion of the 962 for yet another year. A 24-hours without Porsche just would not be the same.

Left
It's 1974, and that 908/03 is back again. The Toblerone car was repainted red, and entered by a team going by the name of 'Ecurie Tibidabo'. Fernandez and Torredemer had a new partner, Bernard Tramont, but the 908 could not repeat its 1973 form, and retired soon after half-distance, with that common Porsche problem, a broken gearbox

Right
In the 1967 Targa Florio, Jochen Neerpasch and Vic Elford drove this 910, chassis number 014, to third place. Seven years on, it was in private hands, and strewn over the Le Mans paddock. From this view of the primitive conditions which existed up until 1991, it is easy to see how the teams now welcome the security and privacy of the pit garages; if nothing else, there will be less thefts of tools, equipment and (no joking) even pieces of bodywork. In 1974 Gérard Cuynet entered this car for himself, Jean-Louis Gama and Yves Evrard; they ran out of fuel

In their Sunday morning edition, the local newspaper, La Nouvelle République, commented as follows on this French-entered car: 'A worry: Robert Buchet's Porsche No.61, driven by Ballot-Léna, is no longer in the leading group.' No, it wasn't. Despite the efforts of the Frenchman and his British co-driver, Vic Elford, the Carrera had dropped to thirteenth position in its class. Everything had been going fine until 6.56pm Saturday, when the car came into the pits for the left rear wheel hub to be changed. The time thus lost cost the car its GTS category lead; during the night, the transmission delivered the coup de grâce. The old paddock at Le Mans could at times produce some quite rustic scenes

Below

Porsche Kremer Racing were still some five years from their first Le Mans victory when they brought this Carrera to the 1974 event. Paul Keller and Hans Heyer shared with Erwin Kremer. Things looked good when they qualified top of their class, but the first hint of troubles to come surfaced when the car had a minor crash – in the pits. Kremer was leaving his pit as Jarier's Matra was coming in, and a collision was inevitable. Fortunately, the damage was slight, and the Porsche was soon on its way. Around 9.45pm on Saturday a piston let go, and that was that

Joest Racing's Porsche 908/03s soon became the best of their type, and Reinhold Joest continued to use them long after everyone else had consigned theirs to museums. Not that his were museum pieces – fourth place in 1975 with this example shows that they were fully competitive. It is interesting to note that this car, the preparation of which had been 'assisted' by the officially absent Porsche factory, had a lengthened tail not unlike that which was used on the works 936s the following year. Joest shared the driving with Jürgen Barth and Mario Casoni, who was at the wheel when, at Mulsanne corner during the night, the car was carved up by one driven by a less experienced pilote. Damage to one front fender and headlight caused delays which could not be overcome

If at first you don't succeed... modify the car again, and come back the next year. In 1976 Joest's 908/03 was even closer in style to the new works 936s, although the quality of the fibreglass work left a lot to be desired. Power was provided by a 2.14-litre turbo-six, not unlike the engines of the works cars, and one could not help but get the feeling that Porsche were trusting Herr Joest to pick up the pieces should both the official 936s fail. They didn't, luckily, for this old 908 could finish no higher than seventh. Ernst Kraus and Gunter Steckkoenig drove, for the team owner had been promoted to drive one of the 936s; the best they could manage in qualifying was a dismal 4 minutes 7.07 seconds, 23rd on the grid

In 1976 this pretty Group 5 Carrera was shared by the little-known équipage of Thierry Perrier (team owner) Guy de Saint-Pierre and M Renier, and qualified with a time of 4 minutes 26.7 seconds. After a pretty average run it finished eighteenth

The JMS-Cachia 'X-Ray car' was cleverly decorated, and beat all the other 935s at Le Mans in 1977. That was the year when 935 customer cars first appeared at Le Mans, and set the tone for several years to come. They were the 'silhouette' cars, and the future apparently belonged to their kind. Claude Ballot-Léna shared this car with American Pete Gregg

Left

At last, the 936s were beaten. Three were entered in 1978, and the best they could manage was second place, behind an Alpine Renault A442B. Car number 5, chassis 936 003, was built to 1978 specification, with the unusual droopy-edged wing as seen here. This was a design developed by aircraft-manufacturer Dornier, and it reduced the car's susceptibility to changes in lift caused by cross-winds. (Photo courtesy Porsche)

Below

In 1978 the Whittington brothers, Don and Bill, entered this 935 in the IMSA category, but retired following a crash. The car advertises Liqui-Moly and Road Atlanta, the latter then owned by the famous brothers; it was not known until much later exactly whence their, er, finance came

Previous year's winners the Kremers returned in 1980, with a fleet of 935s. The pink and white livery of Japanese Italya Sport debuted on this 935, driven by Tetsu Ikuzawa, Axel Plankenhorn, and Rolf Stommelen (guess which one brought the sponsor). The weather that year was not the best, and this Saturday morning view shows that the rain had managed to creep into the Kremers' paddock enclosure

One of the best-loved rituals at Le Mans is the pushing of the cars on to the grid. It takes place well before the off, but signifies that most of the preamble is finally over, and things are really beginning to warm up – even though that term may have been less than appropriate in the midst of the 1980 downpour. Here the works 924 of Barth and Schurti gets the treatment

Bob Akin's pretty Kremer-built 1981 935K4, displaying the Coca Cola paintwork which was typical of his cars. This one was driven by Akin, Paul Miller and Craig Siebert. The overhead view of the car, here taking its place in the pits, shows well the elongated fins above all four fenders, the narrow, high, wing, and the clear aerodynamic fairing which covers the rear window

Below
During the Wednesday evening practice session for the 1982 edition of the race, Harold Grohs had a massive accident at the wheel of this Joest Racing Porsche 935. The car was travelling towards Mulsanne corner when it went out of control, hit the barriers on both sides of the road, and finally exploded as it came to rest. Although the car was totalled, Grohs came to no harm, showing that a sturdy sportscar can provide a safe haven for the driver, provided he is well strapped in – and has a lot of luck on his side

Above
Scrutineering gives the townspeople of Le Mans the opportunity of seeing the cars at relatively close quarters. One of the most interesting features of pesage is the pont elevateur (hoist) which permits a car's undersides to be checked for compliance with regulations. Unfortunately for them, secretive teams face the prospect of having all their hush-hush ground-effect tweaks exposed to the gaze of public and rivals alike. In 1991 this resulted in quite an amusing spectacle: Jaguar mechanics standing shoulder to shoulder around the hoist as their cars rose into the air, whilst the local populace reacted with cheers of glee every time some intrepid lensman managed to poke his camera between the massed wrenches, and steal a flash picture of the Jaguar's underbody. Scrutineering can be fun. For Edgar Doeren's Porsche, in 1982, it was all routine, and the car he shared with Contreras and Sprowls qualified in first position in Group 5. However, it became an early casualty, out of fuel even before Sprowls managed to get a drive

Right

With the arrival of Group C, most teams found themselves having to scratch around to find suitable new cars, for there was little available in the way of ready-to-run customer racers. Joest solved the problem by building a closed coupé around a tube frame 936 chassis, the resulting 936C JR 005 appearing at Le Mans in 1982. 'Brilliant Bob' Wollek teamed with the Martin brothers, Jean-Michel and Phillipe. They were running in fourth place, behind the three works 956s, when the engine gave out, with only 1 hour to go. This picture was taken at scrutineering, held in the Quinconces des Jacobins, close to the Le Mans city centre; in the background can be seen the gaunt rear of the opera house

Left

As soon as Porsche made the 956 available to private entrants, customers flocked to buy them, and at Le Mans 1983 the entry list boasted no fewer than twelve 956s, any one of which was capable of winning. Never before had any front-line type been present in such large numbers. Here Joest's first such car, 956 104, entered under the name of Sorga SA, is unloaded at the circuit, the evening before scrutineering. The Sunday and Monday before the race always hold much of interest, as the teams arrive, and their (often newly decorated) cars are unveiled for the first time. Klaus Ludwig's name was later added to those already painted on the car

PORSCHE ALMERAS
55
LIT
NATIONAL
Georges Péjaudier
MICHELIN
PORSCHE ALMERAS

The engine that changed Le Mans: the original 2.6-litre version of the 956 motor, descended from the 911, and destined to win more Le Mans races than any other engine before or since

Now here's one for the model-makers.
The Brun and Fitzpatrick teams had a
couple of accidental comings-together
during practice for Le Mans 1984.
The scoreline ended up as Fitz 2, Brun 0,
with the Swiss cars decidedly the worse
for wear. Because of a shortage of (very
expensive) body panels, Fitz allowed Brun
to try out some of the former's spares,
to check for a good fit should the need
arise for Brun to use a replacement during
the race. Thus, for just a few moments,
spectators were treated to the sight of a
Warsteiner-liveried Brun low-downforce
car wearing a Skoal-liveried Fitzpatrick
high-downforce nose, a combination
which must, surely, be unique?

Kremer's bought a pair of 956s, this blue Kenwood car being their second, 956 115. Its 1984 driver line-up was first-class, with a former world champion counted amongst their number. The 956 was the first monocoque Porsche racer, and the whole of the rear-end of the car could be removed, en bloc, from the aluminium tub which ended at the rear bulkhead. The removable nose panel was also a significant improvement, for it ended the days of having to patch up a damaged car; it was much quicker and easier to replace a whole panel

Sunday morning at Le Mans 1984 was blisteringly hot, and the author, standing in the pits, found the bright metal fittings on his camera becoming so hot that they were painful to touch. Stetson-hatted Preston Henn brought some American flamboyance to the circuit, and everyone wished him well. Here, with but a short time remaining, Jean Rondeau takes Henn's 956 out from its final pit-stop on its relentless chase after the leading Joest Porsche. After a good, trouble-free run, the car finished second, only two laps behind the Joest car

Only one Porsche 928 has taken to the Sarthe track, but at least it made it there twice. Chassis 840225 first turned up in 1983, and astonished everyone by actually making it to the finish, 22nd overall. The multi-coloured paintwork on this near-standard, road-registered, Group B car had a beautiful pearlescent finish

Conditions in the old paddock, the Parc des Ravitaillements, differed markedly, depending upon the budget of the team. Anyone who saw the Toyota portable buildings, or Joest's oasis, with its artificial grass, its white garden furniture, and its waiter-service, would know how it could be. But, for so many others, the conditions were primitive in the extreme. Out in the open air, one of Michel Lateste's mechanics rebuilds the rear fender flare of the team's 930 turbo, following a collision during practice

The slogan on the nose sums it up: the end of an era. Raymond Touroul's car was the last 911 at Le Mans – but it went there more than once. It was built around a written-off 911SC chassis, dating from about 1983, using whatever parts were available, and including aluminium doors; it carried the unusual chassis number 'Typ 911/16 000 ORIGIN 0068894A'. Its history includes two Jean d'Arc rallies, and in 1989 it was driven to victory in the French National Hillclimb Championship. Add to that, service as a publicity car for the Rallye Paris-Dakar, use as a fun road-car by Lucien-Francois Bernard, and a foray at Le Mans in 1984, and it can be seen that this car has been around a bit. At seventeen minutes before midnight on Saturday, 15 June 1985, its broken engine forced its retirement, and the 911 chapter at Le Mans was closed

Even after Joest sold his old 936C, it kept on coming back for more. Ernst Schuster bought it, and at Le Mans in 1986 finished sixth, just one contentious lap behind the fifth placed Obermaier 956. Co-driven by Siggi Brun and Rudolf Seher, it had minimal sponsorship, and a colour scheme which appeared to be trying to please everybody. (Photo David Cundy)

The 911 is dead; long live the 961. The 911 had gone for good, but much of it lived on (temporarily), in the shape and configuration of the 961, a race-going version of the 959. The only example built first raced at Le Mans in 1986, and, surprisingly, it was totally unsponsored that year. It had four-wheel drive – trust Porsche to get down to the serious business of experimentation whilst playing at racing – but as practice progressed so did the realisation that four-wheel drive was little, if any, better than two; the torque split was progressively changed more and more in favour of the rear wheels. Even with a 27-minute stop to change a half-shaft, Claude Ballot-Léna and René Metge took the car to seventh overall. The first experience with the 961 encouraged Porsche to bring it back in 1987, and this time to find somebody willing to pay for their name to be put on it

HEURES DU MANS ®

A tie-up between Brun Motorsports and the French Formula 3000 team, GDBA, resulted in the former's 962 117 appearing in this striking pastel green livery when it turned up for scrutineering in 1987. De Thoisy was at the wheel when it crashed, at 10.33pm on Saturday

In 1987 this Porsche 962 gave Kremers
a fourth place, the team's best result
since that magic win of 1979. Although
nominally 962 118, this car was built on
one of T C Prototypes' honeycomb
aluminium chassis, which the Kremers
believe were stronger, and therefore safer,
than the official product. This photograph
captures well the hurly-burly of Le Mans's
overcrowded and dangerous pit lane,
where spectators easily outnumber workers;
in 1991 the pit lane was widened, to the
great relief of all (Photo Ken Wells)

For Porsche, 1988 was a year of holding back, and so the works team did not contest the World Championship. The 962s were entered only in Supercup races, and at Le Mans, where three beautifully turned-out Shell-Dunlop 962s made it to the grid. Driver groupings were Stuck/Bell/Ludwig, Wollek/van der Merwe/Schuppan, and the three Andrettis, Mario/Michael/John. Had it not been for the lead car having a minor fuel pick-up problem whilst being driven by Ludwig, its half-lap deficit at the end of the race could probably have been made up, and Porsche would have won another Le Mans. Maybe

The 1988 works Porsches were fitted with the latest version, type 1.7, of the Motronic engine management system, and this gave them the improved power and fuel consumption characteristics they needed to be able to combat the Jaguars. The design of the long tail was also changed, being substantially deeper at the extreme rear to provide lower venturis, as required by changes in regulations

It is an accepted fact that scrutineering is always overcrowded, to such an extent that only at the designated 'photo' location can one take photographs of cars not largely obscured by the populace. So where is everybody? Could it be that such a minor thing as a cloudburst has scared away even the dedicated press photographers, and the scrutineers too? Only Kremer's personnel are to be seen, with their two 962s impeccably finished as Kremers' cars always are, at pesage in 1989

Kunimitsu Takahashi drove Kremer's 962CK6 03 at Le Mans in 1989. Having survived its scrutineering ordeal by water, it succumbed to trial by fire, when, at noon on Sunday, the Japanese driver hurriedly abandoned it at the Dunlop Curve. Fortunately, Takahashi escaped the blaze unhurt. (Photo David Cundy)

The blue and yellow colours of Brun's Hydro Aluminium-sponsored 962 128 matched the ACO's livery, and perhaps gave it the luck it needed to become the only Brun car to make it to the 1989 finish, in tenth position. 128 had been built to IMSA specification, with a single-turbo engine, and was converted to Group C configuration just for this one race. Uwe Schäfer, whose vivid helmet can be seen here as the car passes the signalling pits at Mulsanne Corner, shared with Norwegian Harald Huysman and Frenchman Dominique Lacaud

Below
Brun's 1989 Le Mans assault was the biggest they had ever mounted, for a surfeit of sponsors (how many teams wish they could say that?) compelled them to enter no fewer than five cars, although two of them still used the old Motronic. 962 117, a car with a race history as long as they come, was one of the two, and it was shared by Franz Konrad, Rudolf Seher and Andres Vilarino; it retired at 9.44pm, when the turbo gave up

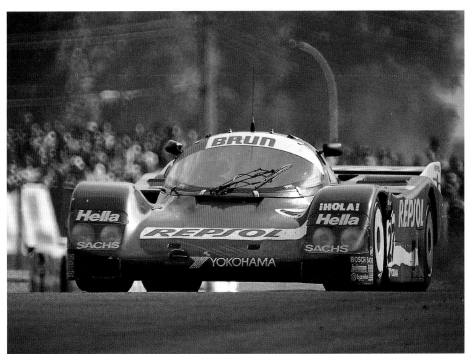

Throughout the 1989 season, one of Joest's 962s, 004, was run in conjunction with Jean-Louis Ricci's 'Ricci Club'. Here the car is seen accelerating away from Mulsanne corner, with the Almeras brothers' ex-Kremer Thompson-chassised 962 110 in pursuit. 004 is another 962 with a long history, and Ricci's team-mates, Henri Pescarolo and Claude Ballot-Léna, have between them more Le Mans participations than any two other drivers. A steady run took them to sixth position at the finish

It was back in the early 1970s that the Japanese first discovered Le Mans, and they have been coming back ever since, in gradually increasing numbers. Using Japanese cars did not appear to be working, so, naturally, they switched to Porsches, the only available customer-cars which gave them any chance of winning. Team Trust have used 956s and 962s since 1983, and in 1990 brought to Le Mans their brand new car, 962 159, but crewed by a Swede, a South African, and, yes, a Japanese, Shunji Kasuya. They finished thirteenth, after a succession of overlong pit-stops to rectify minor faults. The Japanese would have to wait until 1991, and the rising of the Mazda sun, for a Le Mans win

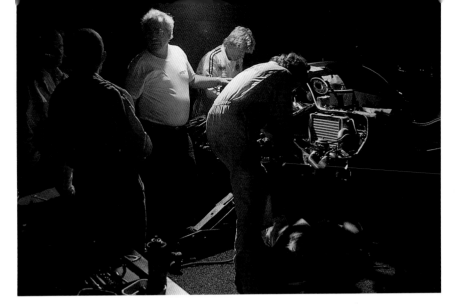

Left
A mechanic's lot is not always a happy one; long hours, difficult working conditions, and long spells away from home soon weed out those who are less than dedicated. With practice finally over, and in the Friday morning darkness just a little after midnight, work continues on Obermaier Racing's 962 902, readying it for Saturday morning's warm-up session. Shared in 1990 by former team-owner Jürgen Lässig, Pierre Yver and Otto Altenbach, this Thompson-chassised 962 ran as reliably as clockwork, to a ninth-place finish

Right
*Team Trust came back to Le Mans in
1991, with the same car as before,
but this time they replaced their Japanese
driver with another Swede. Neither that
nor the car's new colour scheme helped
them very much, and the car retired with
transmission trouble. 1991 was the first
year for the new pit garages, which at
last provided the long-suffering teams
with covered, dry, secure accommodation.
The individual areas are fairly narrow,
but removal of the mesh partitions
between garages allows multi-car teams
to increase their usable work-area*

Opposite
*Night time pit stops are an integral part
of the Le Mans atmosphere, and the
view from the primitive pits-balcony
allowed the public to see what was going
on, in a manner impossible at many
other circuits. Here Tim Lee-Davey's
Schuppan-chassised Porsche has its
engine cover removed — always an
ominous sign — during the 1990 event.
Despite having to have its cooling system
checked at four in the morning, the car
ran through the night and all the way to
4pm Sunday, when it finished 19th.
(Photo David Cundy)*

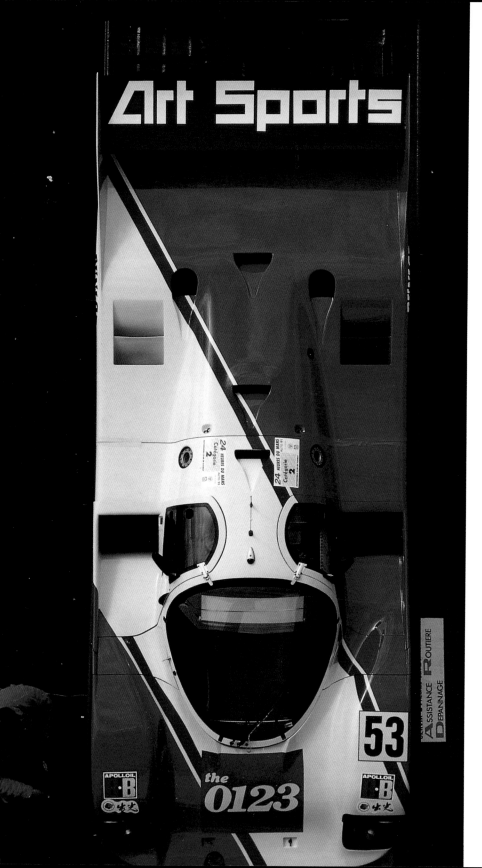

Rarely does one have the opportunity to look vertically down on a Porsche 962, but the walkways between the paddock and the new pit buildings can occasionally provide the appropriate view. When this car went through 1991 scrutineering, it was in plain red livery, and was intended only as Team Schuppan's spare car, not to be raced. Problems with the race cars, both built on Schuppan chassis and featuring new, untried aerodynamics, resulted in the spare (962 146) being painted in race colours of blue and white, and substituting for one of the intended race cars. Hurley Haywood, James Weaver and Wayne Taylor drove it to fifteenth position

The introduction, in 1990, of two chicanes on the ligne droite des Hunaudières, *alias the Mulsanne Straight*, caused such a slowing of the cars that the previous Porsche speciality, the long tail, came under scrutiny. When 1991 came round, all the 962s had switched to short tails, with overhanging or wing-mounted fins, that were routinely used at every circuit except Le Mans. The Obermaier Racing 962 901, of Otto Altenbach, Jürgen Lässig and Pierre Yver, went out with suspension trouble, a problem which afflicted several Le Mans Porsches in 1991; it was almost certainly due to the new regulations, which resulted in the Porsches being ballasted to at least 1000kg, a figure substantially in excess of the cars' design weight

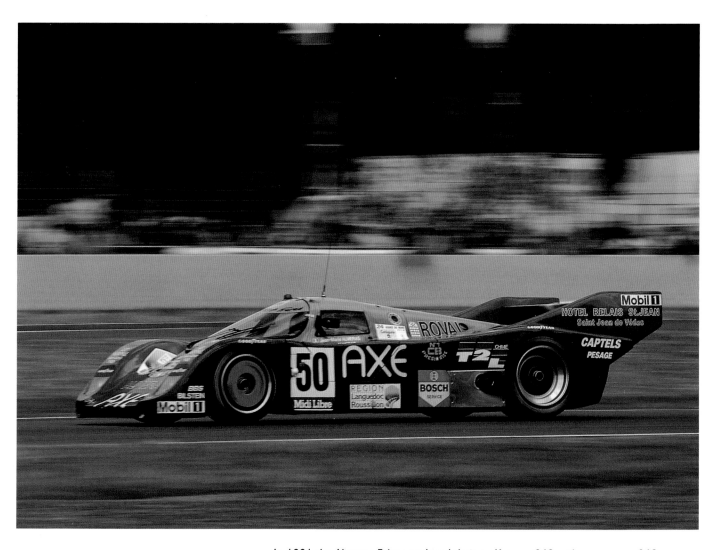

In 1991 the Almeras Frères replaced their ex-Kremer 962 with a new one, 962 001EAF, built on a Thompson chassis. The green paintwork on the top was gently blended into the dark blue lower half, and the car certainly looked nice. Shared by Pierre de Thoisy and team principals Jean-Marie and Jacques Almeras, the 962 eventually crashed

Joest Racing's participation in the 1991 event was not as strong as many had hoped. Three cars were entered, but only two started. Number 58, 962 012, seen here chasing Kremer's 962CK6 09 through the Ford chicane, was driven by Bell, Stuck and Frank Jelinski. The Kremer car, of Manuel Reuter, Toivonen and J J Lehto, shows the special bodywork which Erwin Kremer designed and developed over the preceding couple of years. The faired-in rear wheels are unusual on 962s (although the British RLR team has also used them), and are intended to provide increased downforce. The Kremer 962 finished ninth, the Joest car seventh

PCA Porsche Parade 1990

The USA is big place, and when Americans decide to do something, they usually do it in a big way. Take, for example, the 1990 Porsche Parade. Organised by the Porsche Club of America's Zone 7, the gathering lasted for a whole week, and attracted over 800 cars!

It took place at both the Hyatt Regency Hotel in Monterey, California, and the nearby racetrack of Laguna Seca. Although unfolding at the end of June, the weather was, for the most part, surprisingly cold, despite the sunshine. The Monterey Bay area of California is cooled by winds blowing in from the Pacific, itself having icy currents coming down from the North. An ongoing drought virtually guaranteed a lack of rain, so that despite the restrictions on using water for washing cars, for the most part the competitors in the Concours didn't need to worry about their entries getting dirty.

You might think that a week is a long time to spend playing with Porsches, but nobody seemed to be bored. What with the Concours, sponsored by Porsche Cars North America, which took place on the course of the Hyatt's Del Monte Golf Club, the series of technical instruction courses which unfolded throughout the week, the slalom-based driving tests at Laguna Seca, the Goodie Store, the Art Show, the meals out at the Monterey Bay Aquarium and the historic Carmel Mission, the walking rally, and the opportunity to see lots of Porsches and talk Porsches with people who love them, there just wasn't time to be bored. Organisation of the event was impeccable, thanks to Zone 7's staff working under Chairman Gene Gilpin and Registrars Dave and Lorraine Morse.

Although the Parade is an annual event, and attracts a good number of visitors every year, the 1990 event had a special reason for attracting additional spectators. The Tribute to Porsche at Le Mans was the thing which set this particular event apart from the rest. 1990 was Porsche's fortieth year of competing at Le Mans, and it seemed like a good idea to celebrate that fact, with a parade of historic Le Mans Porsches. Finding examples of each relevant type was not easy, and there were some notable gaps in the line-up; no 906 for example, no 907, 695 or 2000GS. However, what mattered was not what was missing, rather what turned up. Not every entrant was strictly a Le Mans car, and indeed some of the Porsches present had never actually been to Europe, let alone France and Le Mans.

Other entrants did have a Le Mans pedigree, and one of them, the Shell/Dunlop 962, had finished in second place in the 1988 event. Standards of preparation varied, from an almost totally original, unrestored 550, to an immaculate, gleaming 908/80 (alias 936). For all comers there was ample opportunity to take their historic racers on to picturesque Laguna Seca, a hilly switchback of a track which has what every good circuit should have – lots of vantage points.

The first Porsches to race at Le Mans were aluminium-bodied 356 coupés built at Porsche's plant at Gmünd, in Austria. The car shown here is a 1949/50 example owned by Jim Barrington. Although basically similar to the 1951 Le Mans coupé, it lacks the wheel spats which were fitted on the racer. The rear-wheel spats were fairly conventional, and blended smoothly in to the line of the bodywork, but those on the front had to be bulged outwards to provide clearance for the wheels when steering lock was applied

Back in the early 1950s, glass technology did not permit the moulding of large curved areas, so the early Gmünd 356s had to make do with a split windscreen. Porsche should have had two of these cars at Le Mans in 1951, but a succession of accidents destroyed two, so that only a single cobbled-together entry made it to the grid. It also made it to the finish

There was no racing involved, but the Le Mans cars were split into groups according to their performance capabilities, so that as each group took to the track the drivers knew that they would not be mixing it with pilotes of significantly faster (or slower) machinery. Happily, no one came to grief, so the system seemed to have worked well enough.

With the display including such varied cars as 356 Gmund, 911, 924 and 917, one could see the truth in the slogan 'Every Porsche is a Racing Car', a legend which is to be found on the sweatshirt of many an American Porsche-owner. But perhaps the legend should really be 'Every Porsche is a Le Mans car'.

This 356A is typical of the example which finished 13th at Le Mans in 1956. In the period 1951 to 1957, 356s of all types made a total of only nine starts at Le Mans, a surprisingly low figure in view of the record of their successor, the 911

Porsche's first purpose-built sports-racing car was the 550, as exemplified by this car, chassis number 0090. Its general condition, and particularly its upholstery, shows distinct, but not excessive, signs of age, which gives the car a character lacking in many restored examples. 550s last raced at Le Mans in 1959, by which time they had given way to the 718 family

Above

It could almost be the grid for a sports car race on some airfield circuit in 1961, but it's actually the 1990 line up of 550s and 718s at Laguna Seca. In the foreground is the dimpled aluminium of 550 0090, with 550A135 just beyond it. The tail fins belong to an RSK, 718 005, whilst further away can just be seen an RS60LM (718 044) and an RS61, 718 070. In a world accustomed to the razzmatazz of decal-bedecked racing cars which look like mobile billboards, the purity of Porsche's silver spyders makes a refreshing change

Right

The first RSK came along in 1957, and showed that Porsche had learned something about aerodynamics. Note that, at last, the headlamps (here protected by aluminium covers) were carefully blended into the shape of the bodywork, and the nose was extended. This early example, 718 005, is a genuine Le Mans car, its 3rd-place finish in 1958 being the best that Porsche would obtain until ten years later. Drivers in 1958 were Jean Behra and Hans Herrmann

Below
Tail fins like these on 718 005 were used on some Le Mans cars, but when 005 achieved its best Le Mans result they were absent, although sister car 003 was fitted with them for the same race. Opinions differed as to whether the fins really did contribute anything towards the cars' stability, so in the absence of positive evidence fins faded from the Porsche scene, not to reappear until the long-tailed 908s arrived

Previous page
Jo Bonnier and Graham Hill shared 718
044 at Le Mans 1960, but a broken
piston put paid to the RS60's chances.
This was one of two such cars fitted with
slightly overbored (by 0.5mm) engines
which brought their capacity to 1606cc,
bringing them up to 2-litre class

Right
At Laguna Seca, John Webb's American-
liveried RS61, chassis number 718 069,
was a late arrival and, being a non-
runner, did not take part in the track
activities. This car has the aerodynamic
rear fairing which was used from time to
time on some versions of the 718 series,
in an attempt to help the airflow over
the high windscreens which 1960 and
later regulations required to be fitted

Left
The coming of the Carrera GTS, like 904 087 here, saw Porsche at last having a 'modern' – ie mid-engined – racing car, all previous Porsches having been rear-engined, with the powerplant behind the rear axle. Engine was the trusty 1.6-litre flat 4, but apart from that the car broke lots of new (for Porsche) ground.
The chassis for these new 1964 cars was quite different from earlier Porsches; it was fabricated from sheet steel, and featured two substantial longitudinal members, with cross-pieces added where appropriate

Above
The number on George Riley's 904 107 suggests that it was one of the very last 904s (alias Carrera GTS) built, as production amounted to only a little over 100 units. Porsche broke with tradition by using fibreglass bodywork, permanently bonded to the steel chassis, in place of the aluminium used on the car's predecessor, the 718

Left
904s are nowadays looked on as being one of the most desirable of racing sports cars, for they combine superbly pretty bodywork with light weight, good handling and Porsche reliability

Something doesn't look quite right in there. Question: When is a 904 not a 904? Answer: When it's a 906. A handful of 904s were built with six-cylinder engines (the intake trumpets give the game away), and they were renamed 906 and given appropriate chassis numbers, this example being 906 011, owned by Geoff Lewis. The 906 designation caused some confusion when in 1966 Porsche introduced its definitive, and very different, 906 Carrera 6

Left

Bill and Joyce Perrone brought their beautifully restored 910 open coupé to Monterey. The 910 was an aerodynamically-improved development of the 906, and had a short life with the factory team, being used only in 1967. During that year, it was supplemented by the next development, the 907

Below

Most examples of the 910 were fitted with the same 2-litre six-cylinder engine as used in the 906, and there is no doubt that the engine now in this car is a six. However, the chassis number quoted for this 910 is 032, which makes it one of the hill-climb spyders, originally fitted with a 2.0-litre type 771 flat-8, rated at 272bhp

Above
910 007 now belongs to the Collier
Automotive Museum, of Naples, Florida.
This car, driven by Udo Schütz and Joe
Buzzetta, won the 1967 edition of the
Nürburgring 1000km, always one of
Porsche's most coveted races

Right
It's good to see an old-time racer restored
so closely to the condition in which it ran
all those years ago. 910 007 now wears
its Nürburgring livery, including the dayglo
pink identification patch. It also carries its
German licence plate, a feature which
adorned many a Porsche sports-racer
back in the mid 'sixties

Above
Throughout 1969 a green nose-panel on a works Porsche denoted Jo Siffert, the only exception being at the Targa Florio, in which the Swiss did not take part. In 908 025, carrying race number 25, the Siffert/Redman pairing won the 1969 Spa 1000km. 908s were 3-litre flat-8 derivatives of the 2.2-litre 907s, and in various guises enjoyed a remarkably long career, although a Le Mans win always eluded them

Right
At Laguna Seca the Collier Automotive Museum's 908 025 (which debuted at Daytona in 1969) was driven by former Porsche works driver Vic Elford, who gave a fine display of what sports car racing was like before ground-effect came along and stopped tails (long ones, at that) from being hung far out. This car still has the small but controversial rear winglets which Porsche used (with perfect safety) until in June 1969 a CSI edict banned the use of moveable aerodynamic devices. That move can be blamed on the giant collapsing wings which used to fall off Grand Prix cars

Left
Although Porsche themselves never used 908/03s at Le Mans, privateers did, but rule changes (yes, more), ensured that they were ballasted out of contention; light weight had been the 908/03's trump card. Chassis number 010 has been restored to the Gulf livery worn in 1971 by Siffert's car at the Targa Florio (note the trace of Siffert green around the air-intake). Behind the 908, Otis Chandler looks down, perhaps in puzzlement, at a customised 356 spyder which had somehow sneaked on to the grid; it was escorted off before the official photo session took place

Left

Ernst Schuster's progress was delightfully rapid, as he threw the ultra-light and manoeuvrable 908/03 around the Laguna Seca track. Its acceleration out of corners was quite something, too. The short-wheelbase 908 had remarkably responsive handling, and on tight circuits like the Nürburgring and the Piccolo Madonie could run rings around the opposition

Below

The second-place car from the 1970 Rallye Monte Carlo may seem a little out of place at a Le Mans gathering, but at Laguna Seca it served to represent the 2.2-litre Porsche 911ST, a type which saw a lot of action at the Sarthe. Gerard Larrousse drove this car during the Monte, where he was beaten only by Waldegaard's similar Porsche, plated S-T5704

Below
The French team of Porsche Sonauto were the first to enter a 914/6 at Le Mans. The type never had the popularity of the 911, and few ever came to the Sarthe. However, in 1970 this one came, saw and conquered, at least in the GT category. Drivers were the French pairing of Claude Ballot-Léna and Guy Chasseuil. They were placed sixth overall, ahead of the 911s, in a race where only seven cars were classified as finishers. Five of them were Porsches

Above
From a single car in 1966, through a
peak of twenty-four in 1975, to a final,
lone entry in 1985, the 911 was
undoubtedly the most numerous of all
Le Mans cars, regardless of make

Right
Drivers of the Carreras appeared to have
more fun on the Laguna Seca track than
did any other single group, and at times
the 'demonstrations' began to look
suspiciously like races

Whilst pure racing cars tend to have short chassis numbers (some types never get further than '001'), the same cannot be said for roadgoing 911s. This 1974-built Carrera RSR is 9114609040, which in 1975 won its class at Le Mans. It was driven by John Fitzpatrick and Gijs van Lennep, who enjoyed a drama-free event to take a well-deserved victory. The same car, of Georg Loos's Gelo Racing Team, was largely responsible for Porsche winning the GT category of the 1975 World Championships

Jägermeister's brilliant orange livery is one of the most striking ever worn by Carreras, and when turned red by the setting sun it is more beautiful than ever. At Le Mans it was seen not on this RSR, but only on a 934 entered in 1978 by Hervé Poulain

Above

Otis Chandler's gorgeous 917K is a genuine Gulf car, formerly part of the JW Automotive Engineering team. It is plated as 917 004, but its true identity is 917 017; the switch took place in 1970, back at the factory, in what appears to have been a case of making the car fit the paperwork, rather than vice versa. This was Siffert's car at Le Mans in 1970, where it retired after 'Seppe missed a gear; the 917 would happily break a valve or two, if over-revved

Right

A long lens makes Laguna Seca's Corkscrew look even steeper than it really is, but at the wheel of a beast as formidable as a 917 it must seem rather like driving over a cliff. The 917K's flared rear bodywork adds to the impression of immense power, and gives the car a truly fearsome appearance. The style of the marigold stripe across the light blue nose is rather angular, and definitely non-standard

Clearly, this is not Le Mans. The trackside shows Laguna Seca's parched grass which was struggling to survive the 1990 drought in that part of California; by mid 1991 most of this meagre covering had succumbed to the water-shortage. 917 017 is in its 1970 configuration, with deep rear bodywork, small central wing, and no fins. In 1971 it wore new bodywork with a pair of stylish fins, no wing, and shallower rear fenders

The engine bay of Dave Morse's 924 Carrera GT shows the canted four-cylinder turbocharged engine. Everything appears easily accessible, despite the cross bracing, but in racing cars it is essential that time not be lost when carrying out minor adjustments; it's a pity that lessons learned in making racing cars easily serviceable are rarely passed on to their road-car brethren

BF Goodrich-shod cars are probably unique amongst front-line racers in that they always race on road-specification tyres, with the tread suitably shaved to prevent overheating; this should be one good way of ensuring that racing does indeed improve the breed. This 924 GTR, chassis number 008, was raced at Le Mans 1982 by Paul Miller, Patrick Bédard, and Manfred Schurti; at 5.30 am. on Sunday it parted company from its left front wheel, and ground to a permanent halt out at Arnage

This is one of only thirteen factory-built 1979 935s. It has been raced only in the US, and driven only by its owner, Bruce Canepa, who secured good placings at Laguna Seca, Portland and Sears Point. It is in original configuration, and still wears its 1979 bodywork. As such it typifies the 935s which were for several years the mainstay of Le Mans

Above
The Porsche 935 was built to the old Group 5 rules, as a 'silhouette' car. Porsche soon realised that there were some, indeed lots of, loopholes in the regulations. One of these concerned modifications to the fenders, and Porsche took advantage of them to allow for the first time the removal of the high-mounted headlights which have always made it difficult to provide the 911 with adequate downforce at the front. 935s proved particularly popular in US IMSA GT racing, as well as in the European Group 5

MARTINI

SHELL

Turbolader

24-HEURES DU MANS
AUTO
14/15 JUIN 1980
A.S. DE L'AUTOMOBILE CLUB DE L'OUEST DES 24-HEURES

F.I.A. **F.F.S.A.**
Gr6
−2.000
24-HEURES

MARTINI

R. JOEST
J. ICKX

MARTINI
RACING

BOSCH
BILSTEIN
Shell
TEXTAR

Above

When the 908/80 first appeared, its similarity to the 936 was seemingly 100%, but Porsche maintained the pretence that they had not sold any 936s, and that the car was one of Joest's own. Ickx, who shared the driving with Joest, commented that it was exactly like the 936, except for the cigar lighter. Race cars do not have cigar lighters... This view shows clearly the aluminium tubes which made up the chassis in those pre-monocoque days

Left

Dave Morse's 908/80, actually built around chassis 936 004, is essentially a 1980-built 936 with 1977 aerodynamics. It had two tries at Le Mans, and its best finish, second place, was achieved at its first attempt. The eagle-eyed will spot one very tiny flaw in its otherwise perfect restoration: the scrutineering decal on the side of the airbox should show the car as being in the plus 2000 class! These decals usually incorporated a flag denoting the nationality of the entrant, but there is no doubt that in the Le Mans 1980 race the flag decal was absent, just as in this restoration

One notable absentee from Laguna Seca was the 906. The works team used 2-litre 906s only once at Le Mans, but came away with a fourth place in the 1966 event. They outlasted all the Ferraris and were beaten only by the 7-litre Fords. (Photo courtesy Porsche)

956 105 was one of the first batch of customer-956s, built in 1983. Its initial owner was Dieter Schornstein, and it was raced by Reinhold Joest on Schornstein's behalf. Its Le Mans entries netted 4th place in 1983, and 5th in 1984.
Its 1983 entry had actually been in the name of Sorga SA, due to contractual problems which prevented Joest Racing from direct involvement in any car other than the Belga-sponsored 936C of the Martin brothers. It skipped the 1985 race, but was back the next year, this time loaned to Kremers, but it was withdrawn following the fatal accident in which the other Kremer car was destroyed. It was then sold to Walter Lechner, who cannibalised it for parts to build a 962, because rule-changes (!) had outlawed the 956. Eventually, Lechner rebuilt the car, in short-tail configuration, and it was sold to American Jamie Mazzotta, who brought it to Laguna Seca

If you are going to own a 956, you may as well do the job properly, and run a team of them. Jamie Mazzotta's stable includes two such cars, this being the ex-John Fitzpatrick Racing 956 110, which in 1983 raced in the livery shown when on its first outing, Le Mans.
It retired then, as it did the following year, by which time it had been sold to Lord Vestey. Its 1984 Le Mans excursion was under the auspices of Charles Ivey Racing, and 110 wore Rollei's striking livery of silver, white and black

Left
Works 956s always ran in these colours, the blue and white of Rothmans. This is a 956, but rather an unusual one. Although numbered in the works car series, 956 006 never raced for the works team – nor, for that matter, for any other team. It was an unused experimental car, using an especially lightened chassis. It appears to have been fully assembled only after the chassis tests were completed, and it was then sold off, becoming part of the Morspeed collection

One problem with closed cars is that the public can see little or nothing of the driver, and it is often difficult to tell which member of the two-or three-person team is actually in the cockpit at any given time. The 962 was basically little more than an extended-wheelbase version of the 956, and it was designed to meet American IMSA regulations, which required that the driver's pedals be placed behind the centres of the front wheels; the 956 wheelbase was too short to allow this. Eventually, Europe followed the American lead, and the 962 then replaced the 956 in all markets. This is the Dave Morse-owned 962 004, a car with an extensive Le Mans history

962 004 is an ex-Works car which in 1985 debuted at Le Mans, where it was shared by Al Holbert, Vern Schuppan and John Watson. Crankshaft failure forced its retirement from that event. Ickx and Jochen Mass took it to a second place finish at Mosport in 1985, but when in 1986 it returned to Le Mans, it crashed. That wasn't enough to put an end to its career, but when, later that season, it was involved in the Nürburgring pile-up, that really did seem to be it. However, at the end of 1986 it went to Joest Racing, who rebuilt it, and brought it back to Le Mans in 1988. Didier Theys, Franz Konrad and David Hobbs looked after the driving, and the old warhorse finished fifth, in its fourth season of racing!

At the Laguna Seca gathering, Joest Racing Porsches were present in abundance.
Not only that, but a leading member of Joest's personnel was there, 'on holiday'; it was
just like being at Le Mans! Here the Thompson-chassised 962 116 leaves turn five and
sets off up the hill to the Toyota bridge. 116 has been very accurately restored to its
1988 Le Mans trim, with deep rear bodywork

John Winter, Frank Jelinski and Stanley Dickens drove 116 at Le Mans in 1988, finishing fourth. The car had appeared at the Sarthe the previous year, but had quickly fallen victim to the sub-standard fuel which decimated the Porsche ranks that year. This was the only Thompson-chassised car which Joest used; the move to a British-built Porsche had been forced on to the team because at that time the production of Weissach-built examples had slowed to a trickle

Where's everybody gone? Just for a few moments, the bystanders moved away, leaving this three-car 956/962 line-up alone in Laguna Seca's wide pit lane. European racegoers will be envious to note that, in common with many US circuits, there are no pit buildings at Laguna Seca; American tracks do not usually have to contend with European-style weather

When faced with dayglo orange some film has a tendency to turn it into brilliant red, which is pretty but inaccurate. This beautiful and eye-catching orange and white colour scheme is worn by Canepa Racing's 962 HR2. When Porsche 962 production lagged behind demand, Al Holbert's Porsche Motorsports North America was given permission, and even encouragement, to join in the effort by building its own 962s, using factory drawings and parts to ensure complete authenticity. The first one they kept for themselves, but this example was sold to Bruce Leven's Bayside Disposals team, who used it to very good effect in IMSA GTP events. It passed through the hands of Kalagian, and Monarch Sports Systems, before being bought in late 1989 by Bruce Canepa, who then raced it in several Camel GT events

Below
There cannot be many genuine Porsches which have never seen Europe, much less Germany, but this is one of them. 962 HR2 is in spotless condition throughout, and resembles more a show car than a racer. This belies its extensive racing history, for in the hands of Bayside it saw a great deal of IMSA action. Side intakes on IMSA 962s show quite different radiators from those used in Group C; the engine layouts of the two versions were totally different, the IMSA cars being originally single-turbo, with (usually) top-mounted intercoolers, whilst Group C cars were always twin-turbo, with all radiators, except for gearbox cooling, being side-mounted

Overleaf
The complete line-up, under Laguna Seca's clear blue California sky, in celebration of forty years of Le Mans Porsches. At least, it's almost the complete line-up, and certainly it's all anyone got together at one and the same time. The Porsche Club of America's Zone Seven deserves to be congratulated for arranging an excellent meeting

Winners and losers

Porsche slugged away at Le Mans for seventeen years, without having more than an outside chance of coming away as winners. Although they regularly took class victories, the cars just did not have large enough engines to take an outright win. That changed in 1968, for then, for the first time, Porsche had cars which were the equal of anything else on the track. The sport's governing body, the CSI, restricted prototypes to a maximum of 3 litres, although they still permitted large displacement (up to 5-litres) semi-production sports cars to compete.

1968 was, therefore, Porsche's first real stab at the gold. The company entered a grand total of seven prototypes, four of these being 3-litre 908s, the others being the similar but smaller-engined (2.2-litre) 907s. Porsche's driver line-up was headed by the versatile Swiss, Jo Siffert, partnered by Hans Herrmann, who at 40 years of age was something of a veteran. Siffert placed the 908 on pole position, ahead of two similar Porsches and, fourth fastest, the Ford GT40 of Pedro Rodriguez and Lucien Bianchi.

Everybody thought that this must be Porsche's first Le Mans victory; everybody, that is, with the exception of Porsche's engineers, who knew that their alternators were likely to fail at some time during the 24-hours, but who could do nothing to prevent it. For the first four hours of the race, Siffert and Herrmann led. At the end of the fifth hour they were second, bested only by the Ford, but then their race ended, the car falling victim to a broken gearbox housing. Most of the 908s suffered alternator problems which either delayed or stopped them for good, handing victory to the reliable GT40. Two works Porsches finished, a 907 in second position and a 908 in third. If only that Ford had broken...

The following year, Porsche were determined that nothing would go amiss, and therefore provided an even stronger entry than in 1968. Flagships of the white armada were a pair of 4.5-litre engined 917s, at that time the biggest, most powerful, Porsches ever made. Backing them up were three 908 coupés, and a single 908 Spyder. The strategy was for the awesomely fast 917s to outrun the rest of the field and, in the process, break either themselves or any who tried to stay with them. When the carnage was over, the by then very reliable 908s would sweep into the lead, and present Porsche with the company's first Le Mans laurels.

Siffert was there, as was Herrmann, but this time they were in different cars. Siffert had the 908 Spyder, and Herrmann, sharing with Gerard Larrousse, was entrusted with a 908. From the start, it appeared that nobody had told Siffert about the strategy, because he went all out to run with the 917s. It proved too much for the little Spyder, which was pushed away after the gearbox overheated. For Herrmann, however, things were going very differently, and with four hours to go, the plan appeared to be coming together. The 917s had gone, victims of their newness, and only two cars were in with a chance of winning: Herrmann's 908, and a single Ford.

The best laid plans... That Ford was the one which had won the previous year, and in 1969 it was crewed by Jack Oliver and a man whose name was to become synonymous with Le Mans: Jacky Ickx. The final four hours of the 1969 event saw an incredible duel between the two cars and, in particular, between Ickx and Herrmann. On the last few laps they passed and repassed as the hands of the Dutray clock headed towards 2 pm; when they got there, Herrmann's Porsche was 120 metres behind the Ford.

Herrmann was to have one last crack at Le Mans before he retired. And, not surprisingly, it would be at the wheel of a Porsche. By the time June 1970 came around, the once fragile 917s had been honed into strong, dependable and staggeringly quick racing machines. Herrmann, sharing with Dickie Attwood, was to handle one belonging to Porsche Salzburg, whilst Siffert was driving a 917 entered by JW Automotive Engineering Limited, who for the past couple of years had been in charge of a certain well-known Ford. So, the two former team-mates had become rivals.

The weather that year was awful. It rained, on and on and on. Splashing through the downpour, the Porsches held at bay their chief rivals, the 512S Ferraris, one of which with Jacky Ickx amongst its crew, until eventually a multi-car crash near Maison Blanche put paid to the Ferrari challenge. From then on it

Left
Well, it does save having to answer over and over again the same two questions: (1) Is it real or a replica? and (2) What's its racing history? The spelling looks a little odd, but that's the same Hans Herrmann who was still racing (and winning in) Le Mans Porsches as late as 1970. The Holbert is Bob, father of the late Al (himself a Le Mans winner), whilst the two Barths, father and son Edgar and Jürgen, also had excellent sports car racing careers, Jürgen winning at Le Mans in 1977

Overleaf
Porsche 908 number 64 so nearly won the 1969 Le Mans, but was defeated by a matter of 120 metres, in the most thrilling finish ever seen at the Circuit Permanent de la Sarthe. Hans Herrmann and Gerard Larrousse shared 908 031 in its epic duel with the Ford of Ickx and Oliver. Porsche's langheck streamliners had a shape which, more than any other, epitomised speed. It is a pity that the 908 never became a Le Mans winner, for over the years it put up some excellent performances there. However, after 1969 its 3-litre flat-8 just couldn't hope to compete with the 5-litre flat-12s of the 917s.
(Photo courtesy Porsche)

Previous page

At last, at long last, it did eventually all come right for Porsche. In 1970, Porsche 917 023 won, and the years of waiting and trying were crowned with glory. The rebodying of the former long-tailed 917s in the style shown here, dubbed 917K (for kurz, or 'short') had worked wonders in curing the beast of its initially vicious aerodynamically-induced handling deficiencies. Porsche's museum car carries the chassis number of the winner, 917 023, but there is doubt that it is correct. It appears that Porsche, in an astonishing lack of awareness of its own history, actually permitted the Porsche-Salzburg Le Mans winner to be sold to Hans-Dieter Dechent's Martini Racing Team, so as to contest the 1971 season, and subsequently it was sold on again. It is now in the USA, which is where most Le Mans winners end up. This beautifully turned out 917, looking every inch the real thing, is said to be the very first 917 prototype, the unraced Geneva Show car, 917 001. (Photo courtesy Porsche)

was just a matter of which Porsche would win. It wasn't Siffert's; the Siffert/Redman 917 blew its motor when Jo over-revved it, after leading for most of the first ten hours of the race. But, at long last, Porsche had got what they wanted. When, soon after the race, Herrmann announced his retirement from the sport, it was with a Le Mans winner's trophy as part of his collection. It more than made up for the disappointment of the previous year.

In 1971 Porsche won again, courtesy of a 917, Gijs van Lennep, Helmut Marko and the Martini Racing Team, but a Porsche win was not unexpected, given that no works Ferraris were present.

Rule changes have always seemed to affect Porsche more than other manufacturers, and the changes which arrived in 1972 effectively put paid to Porsche attempting more Le Mans wins, at least for the time being. However, they very nearly got another one, almost by accident. Despite the rules at the time favouring 3-litre open sports cars, powered by Grand Prix engines, in 1974 Porsche entered a couple of coupés which were basically Carrera RSR 911s, modified here and there, and powered by turbocharged engines.

The new Carreras were intended as prototypes of the cars which Porsche would build for the forthcoming 'silhouette' championship, in which competing vehicles would have to look like road cars, even though under the skin they might be very different. Although one of the pair retired with engine trouble, the other, shared by Herbert Müller and Gijs van Lennep, astounded everybody by finishing second, beaten only by a single much lighter, more powerful, Matra sports-prototype.

By 1976 Jacky Ickx had joined Porsche, and he used the German cars to extend still further his record of Le Mans victories. Sharing a 936 with van Lennep he won the 1976 event, then in 1977 came back with the same car, albeit heavily modified from its 1976 specification. His co-driver was 3-times winner Henri Pescarolo, but after their 936 retired, Ickx switched to the team's second car, and proceeded to lead the charge from 41st position to attain a commanding lead, Ickx thus gaining his fourth Le Mans win.

Ickx was fast becoming sports car racing's star driver. He returned to the Sarthe in 1978, and was entrusted with the same Porsche with which he had won the 1976 event. Although brought up to 1978 specifications, the 936s could not stay with the new improved Renaults, and Ickx was forced to settle for second position.

Renault, at last having won, promptly withdrew from sports car racing, but for 1979 Porsche once more wheeled out their old and tired 936s; despite the efforts of the drivers, including Ickx yet again, they both retired. Ickx had been partnered by Brian Redman. Although their car was easily the fastest thing on the course, they had too much bad luck. It started with a burst tyre, and ended with that bête noir of 1970s Porsches, an alternator drive belt breakage.

Even with the failure of the works 936s, Le Mans 1979 was no disappointment, for a privately-entered 935 won the event. Porsche Kremer Racing's victory was particularly deserved, because the 935s were undoubtedly slower than the likes

1970 and 1971 really were the years of the 917, which dominated both the Sports Car Championship and Le Mans. Most of the victories – but ironically, not at Le Mans – were achieved by JW Automotive Engineering Limited. Quite satisfied with the 917K, and reluctant to try any aerodynamically-suspect long-tailed variant, JW relented for Le Mans 1971, and raced a pair of factory-prepared langhecke. Jo Siffert and Derek Bell shared 917 045, which like its team-mate suffered a rear-wheel bearing failure, believed to be due to the downforce created by the transverse rear wing; the 1971 langheck clearly had the aerodynamic downforce which the 1969 and 1970 versions lacked. That failure only held back the car, which was leading until eventually halted when the crankcase cracked

Porsche's second Le Mans win was achieved by an experimental 917K, although outwardly it gave no indication of its experimental nature. It differed from other racing 917Ks in having a magnesium chassis frame, the others all being made from aluminium. It was not really expected to win – that honour was surely to go to the longtailed cars – but the failure of the three langhecke left this Martini car of van Lennep and Larrousse running steadily, to achieve a distance record which has never been beaten, and probably never will be. This photograph was taken on the morning of the race, when the Martini cars were going from the paddock to their places in the pits. 1971 was the last year of the 917 coupé, and with its passing ended one of the great eras of sports car racing

of the 936, and the 935, a silhouette car, was clearly derived from the road-going 911 – which had to be good for sales. The Kremer brothers, Erwin and Manfred, had put a great deal of effort into developing their own derivative of the 935, and their efforts paid off handsomely, for they became one of the very few privateers to win Le Mans. Their drivers were Klaus Ludwig and the Whittington brothers, Don and Bill.

Officially, Porsche did not contest the 1980 event, although they provided Reinhold Joest with all he required to build his own 936, which hid behind the designation '908/80'. Joest shared his car with – who else? – Jacky Ickx, and would have won, were it not for gearbox maladies which pushed them back into second place, behind a Rondeau-Ford. By this time, the 936 was getting very long in the tooth, but that did not stop Porsche from dusting off two of the original trio, and lining them up for the start of Le Mans 1981. Ickx and Derek Bell won, and in the process gave the works-built 936s the unusual distinction of having all three cars become winners: in '76 it was 002, in '77 001 managed it, and in '81 it was 003's turn.

For Jacky Ickx, winning Le Mans must be a little boring. When the new Group C rules arrived for 1982, and the 936s were outlawed (how often one needs to say this about Porsches) Ickx and Bell took their new 956, on its maiden outing, to an easy win, ahead of the other two 956s entered. That brought Ickx's win tally to six: four in Porsches, one in a Ford, and one in a Gulf Mirage. It is a total which has not yet been equalled.

The following year, Ickx and Bell were narrowly beaten, but at least it was by another Porsche, the drivers being Australian Vern Schuppan, and Americans Hurley Haywood (who with Jürgen Barth had shared the 1977 winning 936) and Al Holbert. The 956 and its near clone the 962 were responsible for all the Porsche wins from 1982 to 1987, and in the process they took Derek Bell's win record to five, tantalisingly just short of Ickx's. Joest Racing's famous 956, chassis 117, took both the 1984 and 1985 events, (Pescarolo/Ludwig, then Ludwig/Barilla/Winter), joining the 1968/69-winning Ford as the race's only two-time winners, and making Ludwig a three-Porsche winner. In both 1986 and 1987 the successful works cars were crewed by Derek Bell, Hans Stuck and Al Holbert, but then the winning streak ended.

Bell, Stuck and Ludwig came within half a lap of beating the Jaguar which won in 1988, but the biggest drama of all was the 1990 event. Nobody expected a Porsche to be on the front row of the grid, but that's where Argentinian Oscar Larrauri managed to get his Brun Motorsports 962. It was a brand new car, but the 962 was an old design, and it shouldn't have been so fast. However, Larrauri is a trier – some say he tries a mite too hard – and his qualifying achievement is a credit to him. Shortly before the big race, he was involved in an accident in one of the minor supporting races, and by the 4pm start he was feeling distinctly unwell.

The race began, and Larrauri proceeded to put on one of his displays of no-holds-barred tigerish driving. The Brun Porsche immediately showed itself to be

Jacky Ickx's first victory for Porsche came in this Porsche 936 turbo, in 1976, the year that Renault were expecting both the championship and Le Mans to go their way. Porsche's response to the French threat was almost casual, the hastily completed 936 being a hotchpotch of 908, 917 and Carrera turbo parts. Despite that, Porsche won Le Mans and all rounds of the championship. The similarity between this car (with Ickx shown here at the wheel) and the Joest 908/03 from the same year is obvious. 1976 was notable for the weather at Le Mans; Europe was enjoying its best summer for many a year, and the event was hot and dry throughout

The Le Mans paddock used to be exceptionally crowded, with racing cars littered everywhere, trying to squeeze past spectators and in between the trucks which cluttered up the place. It was great. Here Porsche Kremer Racing's 1979 contingent pick their way through the maze as they head for the circuit. The leading car, built up by the Kremers, using their own special modifications, was dubbed the 935K3, and proved to have what it takes; the Whittingtons and Klaus Ludwig won, ahead of a standard 935 which included Paul Newman in its driver line-up. The 935K3 eventually found its way to the Indianapolis Hall of Fame, where it now forms part of a Le Mans car display

the only one of the marque capable of hanging on to the Jaguars and the Nissans. Larrauri, however, was soon exhausted, so for most of the race the driving had to be handled by Spaniard Jesus Pareja and Swiss team-owner Walter Brun. Both good drivers, neither would claim to be in Larrauri's league, but they drove their hearts out to keep that Porsche in contention. Disaster struck when a battery failed, costing a crucial three minutes in changing it.

The 962 charged on, behind just a single Jaguar, until, shortly before the end of the race, the Brun team decided to ease their pace a little; the leading Jaguar, it was believed, was too far ahead to catch, and the Porsche was far enough ahead of the third-placed Jaguar for the Brun crew not have to worry about losing second place. Slowing down was, it turned out, the thing not to do. The pressure was taken off the Jaguar, which had been dangerously close to overheating, but when the Brun Porsche's engine was run at lower, and supposedly more relaxed, rpm, the resulting vibrations dislodged a screw which allowed oil to escape, and the Porsche's engine gave up the ghost, when only fifteen minutes from the flag.

Pareja stopped the car at Mulsanne corner, got out and leaned on the wall of the signalling pits, his head buried in his hands. It was a heartbreaking end to one of the finest performances ever seen in sports car racing.

Above
1983 saw the introduction of a new category of sports car: Group C, which was destined to last, with only minor revisions, up to 1991. The first Group C event at Le Mans was a Porsche pushover, with the first three places all falling to the three works Porsche 956s. This is the Ickx/Bell 956 002, which finished first, and started the 956/962 winning streak which was not broken until 1988

Right
Joest Racing's 956 117, only the second double-winner in the history of the event, rounds the Virage Mulsanne during the Wednesday evening practice prior to Le Mans 1985. Joest's win came as a surprise, not to say a shock, to the works Rothmans Porsche team, who were astonished that a private entrant could outpace the works cars, and use less fuel in the process. Upsets like that have helped to make the Le Mans legend

1987 marked the last appearance of the Rothmans-Porsche 962s, and, for once, they were not wearing numbers 1, 2 and 3. The 1986 championship had been earned by Brun Motorsports, who therefore had the right to use the coveted low numbers, and the Porsche factory had to make do with Brun's old numbers. 962 006 was driven by Bell, Stuck and Haywood, and gave Porsche its last (so far) Le Mans win. In the pits, it shows just how travel-stained a car can become in twenty-four hours. (Photo Ken Wells)

Porsche's official withdrawal from sports car racing did not prevent them from continuing to develop the 962, and providing support to private teams, the principal recipient of assistance being Joest Racing. Their pink car, 962 145, its livery carrying on the tradition set by Kremer's 935 a few years previously, was a contender for victory in 1989, but cooling problems delayed it. A fifteen minute stop to change a water hose put it too far behind to be able to catch up, and the car wound up third, behind a pair of works Mercedes. Winter, incidentally, despite having his name on the car, drove one of the team's other 962s. One has to wonder whether Bob Wollek, who has so often come so close to victory, will ever get that elusive Le Mans win; let's hope so

Menagerie

Porsche's first 41 years of racing at Le Mans have produced more entries than can be claimed by any other manufacturer. Whilst the great majority of those entries were of the standard production or prototype race cars of the day, quite a few of them can well be described as oddballs.

Of all the weird and wonderful Porsches which have ever set rubber on the Circuit Permanent de la Sarthe, perhaps the most memorable was the Pink Pig, alias Big Bertha, aka the Truffeljäger von Zuffenhausen. Beneath its skin (an appropriate term, in the circumstances) the Pink Pig was an ordinary 917. Outwardly, it was something completely different. It was an attempt to combine the low-drag of the longtail Le Mans cars with the handling of the short-tailed sprint versions of the 917 – and it may have succeeded. 'May' is the operative word, for it did not last long enough to prove the point.

It was designed by the Paris-based studio SERA. Appearing for the first time at the Test Days in April 1971, the virgin white car was hailed as one of the ugliest cars to be seen at Le Mans for many a long year. It was extremely fat, its 7'4" width had pronounced side overhang, the purpose of which was to shield the wheels from the airstream, whilst allowing them to be kept free of spats, which can be a very time-consuming nuisance when wheels are to be changed during a pit-stop.

The Pink Pig got its name from the startling livery in which it appeared during the 1971 edition of the 24-Hours. Porsche, aware of the fun being poked at their monstrosity, proceeded to paint the car in porcine pink, then marked upon it in red the dotted lines and names typical of the meat diagrams which adorn the walls of butchers' shops. The truffle-hunter was surprisingly quick, and in the hands of Reinhold Joest and Willi Kauhsen put up a creditable showing, until problems with newly-fitted brake-discs sent it off the road and into retirement. Thankfully, it still survives, and is retained by Porsche, who occasionally display it in their own museum and elsewhere.

After the pig, there was Moby Dick, the great white whale, (see cover), which took to the track in 1978. Moby Dick exemplified Porsche's almost fanatical devotion to the art of producing the car which takes contemporary regulations to their very limit. The car was officially the type 935/78, and was supposedly built to the 'silhouette' formula, which required that cars retain a certain basic similarity to the production models from which they derived, whilst being modified in defined ways.

Moby Dick was Porsche's ultimate expression of this theme. It was meant to look like a 911, and, in a way, it did. The roof – or at least the forward part of it – did resemble that of the 911, and the front hood, windscreen and side-windows also could pass for those of the 911. Those areas apart, the 935/78 was different. Under the pretext of adding wheel-arch extensions (permitted under the then regulations), Porsche provided the car with totally new front fenders,

Right
The Red Lobster was the most extensively modified 935 seen at Le Mans. Basically it was so different from the standard product it wasn't really a 935 at all. IMSA's rather loose regulations applied to entries in the GTX category, where Bob Akin had entered this car, which had been built in America, around a monocoque chassis. Although the engine and the windscreen were of Porsche origin, it seems unlikely that very much else was, but as the car was entered under the name Porsche, it qualifies for inclusion in this volume. Its one Le Mans outing came in 1982, when Akin, David Cowert and Kempler Miller were nominated as drivers. As things turned out, only Akin got to drive the beast, for, shortly after the first hour was up, it spluttered to a halt alongside the Mulsanne signalling pits. It was officially retired at 6.25pm

Overleaf
The innocuous designation 917/20 001 covered the most imaginatively painted car ever to run at Le Mans. Since 1971 there have been lots of cleverly devised liveries, but none could match the sheer cheeky humour of the Pink Pig, alias Bertha-Sau, alias der Trüffeljäger von Zuffenhausen, alias le cochon rose, alias Big Bertha. Originally finished in plain white, the Pig certainly was better received when repainted pink, for then her porcine girth could be forgiven, and she became almost likeable. The result of an aerodynamic experiment, this one-off Porsche raced only at Le Mans, at the big race in 1971 and at the preliminary sessions held in the Spring of that year. The shape certainly worked, but the time left to the 917 coupé was rapidly disappearing, so Bertha was destined to remain without siblings. (Photo courtesy Porsche)

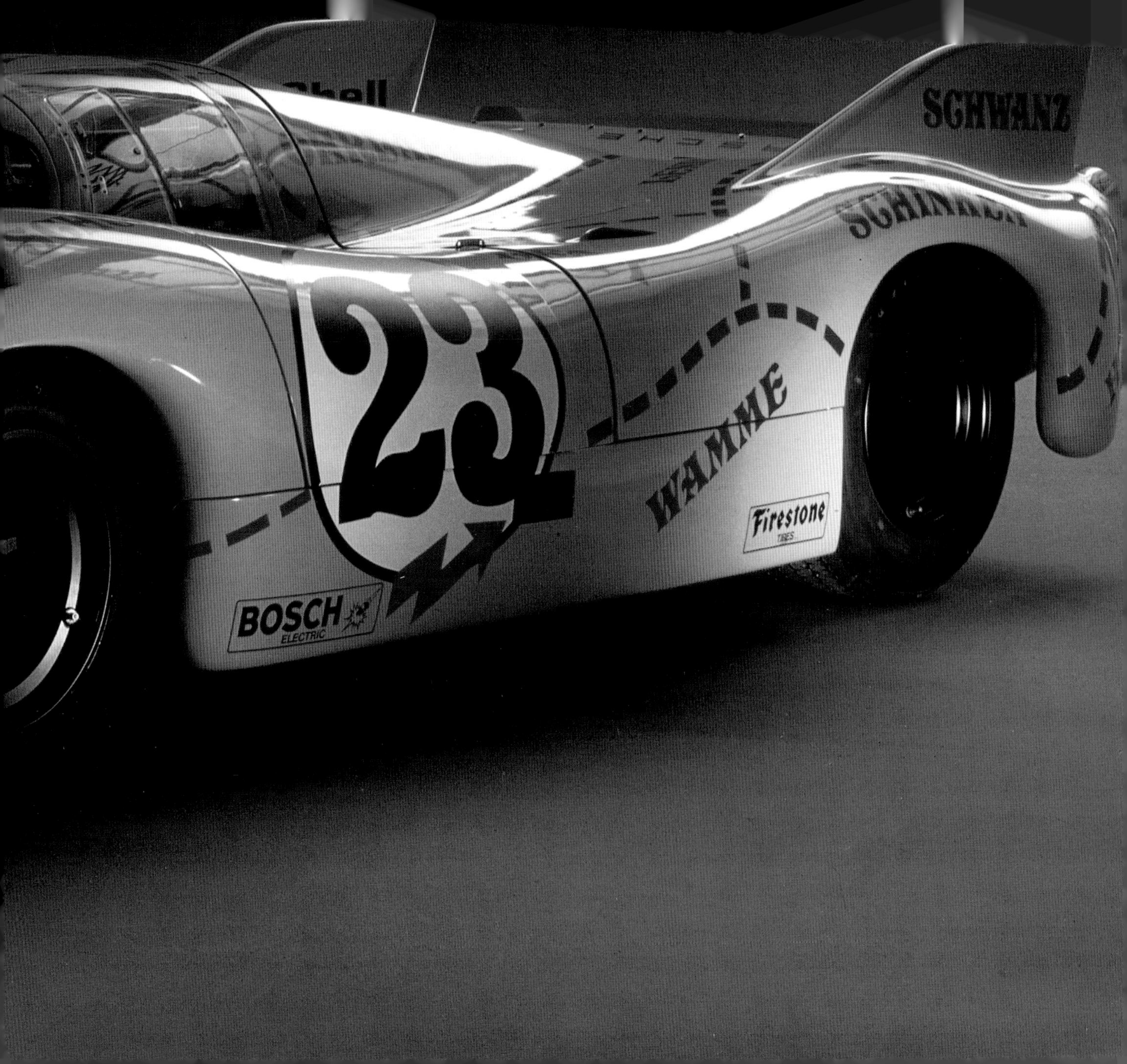
SCHWANZ
23
WAMME
Firestone
TIRES
BOSCH
ELECTRIC

and transverse air-dam. The tail was lengthened appreciably, and the big transverse rear wing carried endplates of a size never seen on a 911. The doors were provided with an outer covering which, at first, linked front fenders with those at the back, until an irate FISA demanded that the fairing be stopped short just a third of the way along the doors. The rear fenders, like those at the front, were also greatly widened, whilst under the skin the car was so heavily modified that Moby Dick wound up being little more than a grotesque caricature of a 911.

The 935/78 was immensely powerful – Porsche reckoned that it had around 750 BHP at its disposal – but a variety of minor ailments slowed it sufficiently for it to be classified 8th at the 1978 Le Mans, one of only four events which it contested.

Where Moby Dick led, another denizen of the deep followed. Le Mans has occasionally let into the ranks of starters cars conforming with IMSA racing categories, and those categories are sometimes rather more liberal in their approach than are their European equivalents. So it was that in 1982 two more extreme 935s took to the track. One of them, entered by John Fitzpatrick, was visually almost a clone of Moby Dick, except that its doors retained the style which had been intended for, but outlawed from, the works 935/78.

The other entrant was much more extensively modified. With sponsorship from, and therefore dubbed, the Red Lobster, Bob Akin's 935 had a front end totally different from any previously seen on any 911 derivative, whilst at the back the tail was redrawn in twin-boom style. The rear wing was very short, but with a substantial chord, whilst the flat, squared-off sides gave the car a boxy look which did nothing for its appearance. The Red Lobster was not spectacularly fast, and it retired from the 1982 event, without having really shone.

The end of yet another era, as commemorated on the wing of Brun's 962 177, the last of the line. Thank you, indeed, Porsche, for four decades of supporting Le Mans; for filling the grids when nobody else could; for making and selling customer-cars when nobody else would; for ten years of the 956/962; for 41 years of sportsmanship. Come back soon

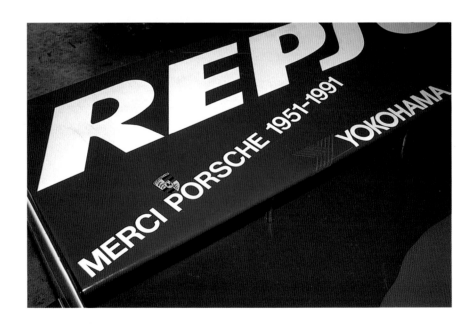